When Sleepy Time is a Happy Time

Written by Leah Puccio   Illustrated by Sarah K. Turner

Halo
PUBLISHING
INTERNATIONAL

ISBN: 978-1-63765-189-6
LCCN: 2022900863

Halo Publishing International, LLC
www.halopublishing.com

Printed and bound in the United States of America

This book is dedicated to Nicholas and Alec.

Nicholas, Thank you for being the best big brother to Alec. For showing him that sleeping in his own bed is not scary and for never wanting to sleep in mommy and daddy's bed because that would have made things even more uncomfortable.

Alec, Thank you for being the best cuddle bug I know and always wanting to fall asleep with mommy. Mommy secretly loved it. I will cherish our nighttime cuddles because every uncomfortable night was worth it.

Jake is four years old and is growing day by day into such a big boy.

Jake looks up to his older brother Johnny and is always trying to keep up with him.

But when it comes to bedtime Jake just will not sleep in his own bed.

Jake gives his mommy and daddy a really hard time and always finds his way back into bed with them.

Then one night a beautiful shining star woke Jake up from a deep sleep.

The shining star grew closer and closer...

In floats a beautiful sleep fairy.

"Hi Jake, my name is Ellie. I stop by the homes of little boys and girls and show them what happens when everyone goes to bed."

Jake looks around and sees his mommy and daddy are sleeping, but they do not look very comfortable.

"Come on Jake let me show you."

Ellie leads Jake over to Johnny's room.

"Jake, look how happy everyone is. Let's go check out your room," says Ellie.

11

Jake looks in his room where everything looks so sad.

"Why are all of my toys so sad?" Jake asks.

"Because you do not sleep with them at night," Ellie says.

"Come on Jake, let me bring you back to bed. Everyone is going to wake up soon."

"Rise and shine!" Jake's mom says, while everyone starts to wake up.

The next night, while everyone is getting ready for bed, Jake tells his mom that he wants to try and sleep in his bed tonight to see if he likes it.

"Jake, that is a great idea," says his mom.

Jake's mom tucks him into bed and reads him a goodnight story.

She kisses Jake on his forehead and tells him how proud she is of him for wanting to try and sleep in his bed like a big boy.

Jake tosses and turns a few times and then falls asleep.

In the middle of the night, he wakes up and thinks about going to sleep with his mom and dad.

He remembers how uncomfortable it would be for everyone if he did.

Jake looks around his room and sees all of his toys and how happy they all are.

Jake gets up and runs to his brother's room to see if Johnny and his toys are just as happy.

Then Jake runs to check on his mom and dad and sees the same thing.

Everyone is so happy.

Jake thinks about jumping in bed with them, but then remembers what his room would feel like if he did...

23

Jake turns around, runs to his room, jumps in his bed, and tells himself he can do it.

He can sleep in his room like a big boy and make his toys and family happy.

Jake lays down and falls back asleep.

"You did it," his parents said.

"You slept in your room all night just like a big boy!"

Jake was so proud of himself, but he realized he did not do it only to be a big boy...

He did it because he wanted sleepy time to be a happy time for all.

CPSIA information can be obtained
at www.ICGtesting.com
Printed in the USA
LVHW070414050422
715321LV00002B/15

9 781637 651896